GLACIERS

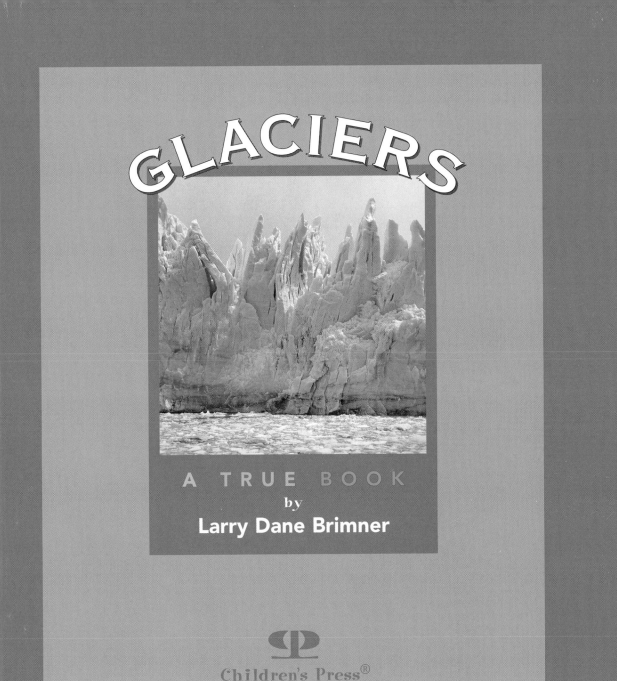

A TRUE BOOK

by

Larry Dane Brimner

Children's Press®
A Division of Grolier Publishing
New York London Hong Kong Sydney
Danbury, Connecticut

A hiker looking
into a crevasse

Visit Children's Press® on the
Internet at:
http://publishing.grolier.com

Subject Consultant
Peter Goodwin
*Science Teacher, Kent School,
Kent, Connecticut*

Reading Consultant
Linda Cornwell
*Coordinator of School Quality
and Professional Improvement
Indiana State Teachers
Association*

Author's Dedication:
*For Debbie and all my friends
at Carpenter Elementary in
Midland, Michigan.*

*The photograph on the cover
shows a glacier in Canada.
The photograph on the title
page shows the edge of
Perito Moreno Glacier
in Argentina.*

Library of Congress Cataloging-in-Publication Data

Brimner, Larry Dane
    Glaciers / by Larry Dane Brimner.
        p.   cm. — (A True book)
    Includes bibliographical references (p.).
    Summary: Describes what glaciers are, how they are formed, and how
they move and shape the Earth.
    ISBN 0-516-20670-2 (lib. bdg.)   0-516-27191-1 (pbk.)
    1. Glaciers—Juvenile literature. [1. Glaciers.] I. Title. II. Series.
GB2403.8 .B75 2000
551.31'2—dc21   99-058047
                                                                      CIP
                                                                      AC

GROLIER
PUBLISHING

© 2000 by Larry Dane Brimner
All rights reserved. Published simultaneously in Canada.
Printed in the United States of America.
1 2 3 4 5 6 7 8 9 0 R 09 08 07 06 05 04 03 02 01 00

Contents

A mountain glacier at Glacier
Bay National Park in Alaska

Rivers of Ice!

Glaciers are huge, slow-moving "rivers" of ice and snow. They flow down from mountain peaks and spread out across nearly flat lands. Some make it to the sea just like rivers of water. Others begin to melt in the warmth of lower elevations, becoming streams of meltwater.

Only the tips of mountains stick out from this ice cap in Alaska.

Glaciers are found on every continent except Australia. Some are so big that they spread over entire mountains and plains. Huge glaciers called ice caps are so thick that they almost bury mountains. Larger still are ice sheets, which blanket vast areas of continents. Ice sheets cover much of Greenland and Antarctica. In fact, Antarctica—which is twice the

The edge of the Greenland ice sheet

Most of the world's supply of freshwater is frozen in glacier ice.

size of Australia—is covered by the world's largest ice sheet.

Much of the Earth is covered by water—salty seawater. Barely 3 percent of the Earth's water is freshwater—the kind of water we drink. Glaciers are natural reservoirs of freshwater. More than three-fourths of our supply of freshwater is frozen in glacier ice!

How Glaciers Form

Snow falls. It collects in hollows and deep valleys. In some places in the world, the snow never melts entirely. Then new snow falls on top of the old snow. Year after year—sometimes for tens of thousands of years—snow piles deeper and deeper. Its weight presses

In areas where glaciers form, more snow falls each winter than melts each summer.

down and squeezes the air out of the layers beneath.

These lower layers of snow become packed down and turn into ice. The ice becomes heavier as it becomes thicker.

Then, slowly, like an ice cube on a slanted surface, the ice and snow begin to flow down-hill. A glacier has formed.

The weight of so much ice and snow causes a glacier to flow downhill.

Glaciers most often occur at high elevations and are made up of three distinct layers. The top layer is snow. The next layer is a grainy mixture of snow and ice, called névé. Beneath that is a layer of solid ice. These layers form glaciers that are sometimes several hundred feet thick, but glaciers can be much thicker. In places, glacial ice in Antarctica is more than 15,000 feet (4,572 meters) thick!

In Antarctica, glacial ice can be hundreds or even thousands of feet thick.

When ice builds up to a thickness of about 60 to 80 ft. (18 to 24 m), it begins to move downhill under its own weight. This great weight also gives the ice a quality that scientists call "plastic flow"—it allows the ice to bend and flow over the uneven surface beneath it.

But the ice can do this only as long as its movement is slow. If its movement is too quick, the ice breaks and great, deep cracks, or crevasses, are created. Crevasses are also created when the ice turns corners or flows over ledges. Because the top layer of the

Crevasses form when the glacier moves over mounds or when the slope suddenly steepens (left). These people are hiking beside a crevasse (below).

glacier is not under pressure, it is still stiff and cannot stretch over the curves, so it cracks.

Meltwater trickling down through cracks in the ice can help a glacier slide downhill.

Glaciers in warmer, or temperate, regions have another way of moving. When a glacier presses hard against underlying rock, the great weight causes some of the ice to melt. During the summer months, meltwater trickles down through cracks in the ice. This layer of water under the glacier helps the glacier slide downhill.

Uphill, new snow feeds glaciers and helps them to grow. Downhill, it's another story. If a glacier reaches an elevation where the temperature is warmer, its end, or snout, begins to melt. If a glacier reaches the shoreline without melting, it

If a glacier reaches a warm enough elevation, its snout begins to melt (right). In colder parts of the world, a glacier may reach the sea without melting (below).

breaks off into the sea. When there is little new snow or unusually long warm periods, glaciers slowly retreat, or shrink.

Shaping Earth

Glaciers help shape the Earth. Some scientists have described them as "nature's bulldozers." This is because glaciers do not just slip downhill. On the way, they push, pull, and pluck at the rocks underneath them.

When a glacier begins to form in a mountain hollow, it

Glaciers drag rocks and rubble with them as they move downhill.

carves out a round basin called a cirque. It does this over many seasons of freezing in winter and melting in summer.

The cirque begins to form when meltwater seeps deep into cracks in the mountainside. But water expands, or gets bigger, when it is frozen. So when the meltwater freezes again, it presses against the sides of the

A cirque

cracks. Chunks of the mountain-side eventually break away from the mountain to form the cirque. The loose rock is carried away by the glacier.

When cirques form on all sides of a mountain, they leave behind a jagged, pyramid-shaped peak, called a horn, that is common to landscapes shaped by glaciers.

Glacial ice also freezes onto the rough rock surface beneath it. When this happens and a

The Matterhorn, in Switzerland, is a good example of a horn.

glacier moves on, it carries with it rocks of all sizes that it has plucked from the surface. This process is called gouging.

Rocks of all sizes are carried with a glacier as it gouges the Earth's surface (left). Valleys carved by glaciers are U-shaped (right).

In turn, the rocks in the glacier grind against rocks on the Earth's surface as they are carried downhill, helping to carve out the U-shaped valleys that are typical of glacial sculpting. In contrast, valleys shaped by rivers are V-shaped.

As the rocks grind against one another, a fine powder, called rock flour, is created. Rock flour sometimes colors glacial meltwater in shades from milky white to murky brown.

The meltwater of a glacier is often colored by rock flour.

A side, or lateral, moraine

Other rocks wear away, or erode, and fall to the sides of a glacier, forming ridges of rock and rubble called moraines. Often, a main glacier will be joined by several tributary, or side, glaciers. This creates a

Dark bands of moraine show where many glaciers have joined into one.

larger glacier with multiple moraines. The moraines can streak the glacier like curvy parallel raceways. What happens when the ice melts? The moraines are left behind to form curvy parallel hills.

An end moraine

As a glacier moves downhill, it also pushes rock debris in front of it. This debris, called end moraine, may get bull-dozed into a curved barrier at the end of the glacier. This barrier may eventually hold back a lake filled with ice-cold meltwater.

Moraine Lake in Canada is a glacial lake held back by an end moraine.

Valleys High and Low

Sometimes a side glacier joins a main glacier at the upper level of the main glacier, long after the main glacier has carved a deep valley for itself. After the ice melts, the valley carved by the side glacier is left high above the valley carved by the main glacier—so it is called a hanging valley. Hanging valleys often have spectacular waterfalls, such as Yosemite Falls in the United States.

A fjord in Norway

Yosemite Falls

Some glaciers gouged their valleys right down to sea level and even below it. Then the glaciers melted and the sea levels rose, filling these valleys with sea water and forming fjords, or inlets. Some fjords are more than 4,000 ft. (1,219 m) deep!

Icebergs!

A glacier that reaches the sea does not stop. It continues to flow—off the land and into the sea! There, it floats as a thick slab of ice, or ice shelf, but remains attached to the main glacier.

Icebergs form when large chunks of ice break away from

An ice shelf in
Alaska (left); a glacier
calving (above)

the ice shelf, a process called
calving. Carried by ocean currents, which are like rivers within
the oceans, the chunks become
islands of ice drifting on the sea.

Most of an iceberg lies below the water.

Some icebergs rise 200 ft. (61 m) or more above the water. Some are flat. Others are jagged. The largest icebergs are several miles long—truly floating islands. The part of an iceberg that people see above water is only a small part of the story, though. More than three-fourths of an iceberg lies beneath the ocean's surface.

As a result, icebergs pose a threat to shipping. When currents carry them out to sea, icebergs sometimes drift into routes used by ships. Many icebergs from Greenland travel all the way to the Grand Banks, a spot off the coast of Newfoundland. Sailors

"Iceberg Alley" (above) is near Newfoundland. In some areas, specially equipped "icebreaker" ships escort other ships through iceberg-filled waters (right).

call this area "Iceberg Alley," and they know they need to be alert when sailing there. An iceberg can easily rip open the steel hull, or bottom, of a ship.

Today, sailors can avoid icebergs. Patrols are on constant lookout and advise sailors about their locations. Before there were patrols, however, many ships sank when they hit an iceberg. Between 1882 and 1890, fourteen ships sank and another forty were damaged in Iceberg Alley. But after the *Titanic* hit an iceberg and sank in 1912, patrols began mapping the positions of dangerous icebergs to keep ships safe at sea.

The Titanic

When the *Titanic* set sail from Southhampton, England, bound for New York on April 10, 1912, no one imagined the voyage would end in terror and sadness. After all, the huge ship was a shining example of twentieth-century progress and everyone said it was unsinkable.

But on the cold night of Sunday, April 14, disaster struck. The *Titanic*, carrying more than two thousand passengers and crew, crashed into a looming iceberg that ripped open the ship's hull. When it sank, the *Titanic* carried more than fifteen hundred passengers to a cold, Atlantic grave.

An artist's impression of the sinking of the *Titanic*

The iceberg that struck the *Titanic*

Ice Ages

At various times in the Earth's history, the climate has been much colder than it is now. During these cold spells, or ice ages, the polar ice sheets advanced. They joined with other glaciers to cover much of the Earth. Indeed, some scientists think that during

Woolly mammoths (top) lived during Earth's most recent ice age. During an ice age, much of the Earth might look how the Antarctic looks today (bottom).

one ice age, ice may have covered most of the Earth. Today, we are in an interglacial period—a time of warming.

What causes ice ages? Scientists believe they are due to the Earth's orbit (its path around the sun) and tilt, which don't always stay the same.

Scientists believe ice ages occur when Earth's orbit takes it farther away from the sun than usual. This reduces the amount of the sun's heat that reaches our planet. At the same time, a slightly different tilt makes the poles even colder. And the ice sheets advance.

We can see the effects of a glacier long after the glacier has melted away.

The Earth is always changing. The most recent ice age ended about 10,000 years ago. If history repeats itself, there will probably be other ice ages— but not for thousands of years.

To Find Out More

Here are some additional resources to help you learn more about glaciers:

Books

Bailey, Ronald H. **Glacier.** Time-Life Books, 1982.

Bramwell, Martyn. **Glaciers and Ice Caps.** Franklin Watts, 1994.

Nixon, Hershell H. & Joan Lowery Nixon. **Glaciers: Nature's Frozen Rivers.** Dodd, Mead & Co., 1980.

Organizations and Online Sites

Glacier
http://www.glacier.rice.edu/

Information about glaciers and about living and studying in Antarctica.

Glacier National Park
National Park Service
P.O. Box 128
West Glacier, MT 59936
http://www.nps.gov/glac/index.htm

Glacier National Park includes several small alpine glaciers formed in the last few thousand years. Its website tells about the geologic history of the park.

Glaciers and Glacial Ages
http://www.uvm.edu/whale/GlaciersGlacialAges.html

Find out how glaciers form.

Important Words

barrier something that blocks the way or stops movement

cirque hollow on a mountainside where a glacier first forms

debris scattered fragments or rubble

gouging scooping out

ice cap dome of ice filling in and covering a large area of land

ice sheet huge ice cap; ice sheets are the largest type of glacier and cover large parts of Greenland and Antarctica

moraine rocks, rubble, and grit carried along by a glacier and dropped in front of or to the sides of the glacier

multiple more than one

temperate regions that have warm dry summers and cool wet winters

Index

Meet the Author

Larry Dane Brimner is a former teacher who now writes full-time for children. His titles for Children's Press include *The World Wide Web*, *Polar Mammals*, and *The Winter Olympics*, among others. He lives in the American Southwest, but can most often be found in cyber-space at *ldb@brimner.com*.